# Together is
# Better

Eddie Jaroul Harris

Copyright © 2018 GBRTGalaxy Puiblishing,
Eddie Jaroul Harris & Success Definers
All rights reserved.
ISBN: 1719230226

## TABLE OF CONTENTS

Acknowledgments     i

| | | |
|---|---|---|
| 1 | Broke Together or Rich Alone | Pg. 4 |
| 2 | Lonely How I Like It | Pg. 14 |
| 3 | Learning a New Way | Pg. 21 |
| 4 | Values & Virtues | Pg. 37 |
| 5 | Culture | Pg. 41 |
| 6 | You are in Control | Pg. 48 |
| 7 | Bring them Out | Pg. 55 |
| 8 | Joy is Currency | Pg. 61 |
| 9 | Representing | Pg. 70 |
| 10 | Conclusion | Pg. 80 |

# **Acknowledgement**

Special thanks to my families

Brown, Harris, Gray, Hatchett, Joseph, Johnson, Davis, Exodus, Van Harris, Yachdiel, Pitcher, White, & Vaughan

My love and biggest fan the strong one out of the bunch Breanne.

Thanks for the support!

My lovely Mother & My Queen Deloris Davis

My Father, Coach & Mentor Zach Sr.

My backbone and strength Samuel and Jamell.

My closest comrades Jason and Zachary

My counselors Mom and Pops Vaughan

My first teacher Anthony "Wu Leo" Malik

My spiritual advisor Tylor "Guru"

The light in my galaxy Naomi

My elder Brother – The Head of the Tribe Eshua

I would not be here if it wasn't for a young lady who allowed me to guide her on her journey.

Miss Taniya Stacy Harris.

My world became real when I held and kissed my young Queen, and everything made since on 2-12-14. Thank you Akylah Asa for arriving when you did. You saved me.

You are your mother's baby, but you most certainly are daddy's man. The youngest in our tribe and refuse to get left behind even if you must cry a little to get where you are going. Your name is aggressive for a reason.
Never settle Keelyn.

Love you all!!!

Enjoy my thoughts. I wrote them out for you!
If I did not mention you above believe that you are an important part of my journey and most likely the inspiration behind the words on these following pages.

# TOGETHER IS BETTER

## Chapter 1

### Broke Together or Rich Alone.

Would you rather be broke together or rich alone?

Being rich with family is one of the things that we tell ourselves and our children. For African Americans, when we are not able to afford the lifestyle that we envisioned, this becomes the ultimate consolation prize. This gives us a focus on family and not on the accumulation of things. It brings a closeness that we carry with us for our entire life.

The problem arises for us, as individuals, when we allow this wonderful gift bestowed upon us to be a driving force in our lives that can prevent us from financial independence and wealth generation. The goal is to be able to turn family into a profitable situation. Being rich with family means that there is trust and loyalty between the members of that family. The only thing needed to go from rich with family to having a rich family is mind frame. This is our journey throughout this book. It is not necessary for us to recreate the "wheel". In fact, nearly every other community around the world has made this a very normal part of their culture. Every young black entrepreneur must guard against the feeling of "making money off of our people". You make money when you do business. It is a necessary part of the process. So, why are we iffy on making money "off" of each other when this is a natural occurrence in every other community?

A 2018 report from Nielsen on the current buying power of consumers of color offers a fascinating look at how we're spending our money. While African Americans make up just 14% of the population, we are responsible for some $1.2 trillion in purchases annually. Nielsen's research shows that 38% of African Americans between the ages of 18 and 34 and 41% of those aged 35 or older expect the brands they buy to support social causes, outpacing the total population by 4% and 15%, respectively. The money is there. The people are spending. I would venture as far as to say they want you to take their money in exchange for great products and exceptional customer service.

Many of us have a notion in our mind that it is lonely at the top. As if making money somehow isolates you from the people that you love. I would offer a counter argument: It is lonely at the bottom. Think of the times when you felt most alone and lacking that support you wanted. For me, it was when I needed financial assistance from others.

Refusing to reach a certain level of financial security because you feel as though you would be leaving behind friends and family is not only the wrong way to go about the issue, but it is also a major contributor to the problem. The problem being poor economics in your family and community. The move is for you to figure out how to work with, work for, and provide work for, family and friends. Understanding this is by a wide shot easier said than done, especially when members of the community can attribute one who succeeds and focuses on change as "selling-out". But, it does take two to tangle. The drive to become better is filled with near compulsive-like behavior. Long nights are followed by grueling shifts at day jobs in pursuit of getting ahead and living the dream. Many entrepreneurs lose touch with family simply because of the large amount of time required to succeed in this American market.

Relationships are pushed to their brinks as would-be entrepreneurs plead with family and friends to be patient with them as they chase a dream they claim as their own. Children often feel as if mom and dad are ignoring them. Spouses are left lonely. Cousins and brothers wonder why you never come around and hang out anymore. You are giving every waking moment of your time to your dream. Every ounce of passion is spent on promoting your business. You are dedicated to learning your industry and your dedication is laser sharp on being a success. That same fervor needs to go into the educating of family and community. Because without you explaining and communicating your journey others are left to fill in the gaps on their own.

Time, passion, dedication spent with your supporters during the incubation of your business will be a win -

win for you and your business. It is also beneficial for family.

One of the first things that need to happen to a person who wants to be their own boss or affect change in their community is a self-audit. Self-auditing involves looking at all your skills – your soft skills as well as your career-based skills. Soft skills are personal attributes that enable someone to interact effectively and harmoniously with other people. This is a very important part of the process because to make the proper change you must have a clear understanding of the tools you have at your disposal.

Now, if we could take self-auditing to another level and do a family-audit that would be monumental. For example: Auntie so and so who enjoys throwing parties is a natural at bringing people together. She may not be the best person to have conduct an important business meeting, but she is an amazing party planner. Having her operate well within her skill set improves your potential output and expands your toolbox. By placing people in positions that allow them to succeed with ease, you will succeed with them.

We must begin to remove the idea from our consciousness that being financially insufficient, or for better terms "broke", is some sort of badge of honor. It is not. It is not "keeping it real". I have heard that people sometimes assume that a black person that "makes" it, does so by kissing up or having a slave like mentality. That is not a helpful way of looking at someone who has worked hard to put themselves in a position to feed their family. It breeds resentment. I wonder why no one thinks that a white man who works for a black man is a kiss up? Let us build bridges with each other. Everyone has their path to travel and none is better than the other. God gave us all customized maps. Your compass is the one that your family and community gives you through morals and values instilled in childhood. It is time to start your journey.

It is not noble to be a representation of a label that was fabricated and thrust upon you and your community even before you could speak. The label being that somehow an entire group of people are financially inept. I need to clarify that if you find that you have little to no money and you are a happy individual and all your basic needs and your family basic needs are met, this may not apply to you. There are no absolutes.

Yet, if you are struggling to pay bills and find yourself unhappy or generally in a bad mood over finances, your financial situation, or your career prospects. Then this is your book. Also, let's not forget that an adult takes responsibilities for their actions and the consequences of those actions. Be careful to not give your pen to someone else to write your story. You have choices and control over some of the things in your life. Focus on the things that you can control and trust the process on the things that are out of your control.

When I was down on my knuckles, I knew that the change I wanted would have to come from somewhere deep inside me. I was drinking every morning or enough mornings for me to say it was too often. I had found myself in front of judges and risking my freedom in the court systems from making bad miscalculated decisions. I was not working or generating income in a way that could contribute to my living situation. I thank my brother who made it his personal responsibility to step into my life and support me. In this depressed state I was unmotivated. I was simply down. My brother could not motivate me. Neither could my mother or any friend. I knew I could not become financially stable with the mind state that I had. I had every excuse and it wasn't until I removed them and looked up from my pit of darkness did I have my vision shown to me. In that moment I refused to stay broke or be broken. And so, my ascension began.

The most successful people focus on the goal and remove the things that can detract from the end goal or distract them in their pursuit. It was a harsh reality for me when I realized that the detractor was my own guilt and low self-esteem. The main distraction was my favorite vices; drinking and hanging out mostly. What would I become if I could not be the person that hid amongst the lost ones for so long? If I was forced to face my reality and accept my role in the living hell that I had created for myself. The answer in the shortest way I can answer it is: great. I would become great. And the scariest thing for a broken person is the prospect of becoming great. Why? Psychologically one of the core fears of success is that the change that comes with it will lead to loneliness. I dare you to face that reality and not blink. Loneliness! But we talked about that already. It is way lonelier at the bottom. It is time to rise and be great.

So, for me, the growth looked like taking jobs at gas stations and gyms, reading books and enrolling in YouTube University to study videos and lectures of the great motivators, seeking mentors and any opportunity to provide a service for others. This is how I turned my thinking around. I began cleaning up debt and correcting past mistakes. I focused on being intentional in my relationships by removing the toxic ones and cultivating the ones that brought value. I mentored others as I sought out mentors for self. I taught others as I was being taught. I tried many forms of learning and growth and to this day I still try new ways to learn, unlearn, and relearn what I think I know about this journey called life.

Rich with family is a great second place prize in the competition of life. But why not be rich AND rich with family? We must actively begin the process of shedding old ways and embracing new beginnings.

## Chapter 2

### Lonely How I Like it.

If you want to be strong, learn to love being alone

We as Americans have a fondness for the struggle. It runs through our music and through our stories as a necessity of life. Even our interpretation of some of the holy scriptures seems to confirm God's fondness for the plighted ones. But this type of "favor" supposedly blessed upon us from our maker rarely manifests into economic sustainability and/or community growth. Not for nothing, many successful people give credence to their early life struggles as fuel for their ultimately unimaginable wealth and success. So how do we go from pain and struggle as a hindrance to utilizing its motivating factors as fuel?

Learning to love the person you are and the community you are from is important. If being alone makes you strong it must be because being alone is one of the most difficult things to deal with. The human brain developed over time. It's not because we were just becoming more intelligent. Science says our brains grew because we needed to be able to handle complex social structures; the developing levels of communication that came with growing families and tribes for instance. We became more intelligent when we developed the brain power to learn, share, and interact with others. It is kind of interesting that we literally developed and matured into the state we are in today to be able to deal with the thing that we tend to shy away from most, and that is the human interaction. But there is a silver lining. If you take some time to be alone and learn to find your voice, you will most certainly become a better communicator and develop the ability to make the impact you envision for your community.

If you take a small stroll on the social media highway you will quickly find many people who feel as though they do not receive enough support or see a lot of things like the famous "I made myself hot" quotes. If there are so many people who are self-made and who are not in need of any assistance, then why are there also so many people who are complaining from the lack of support from their family and community? The thing is, we have lost our ability to communicate effectively with each other. We expect that the strongest of us rose from the mud and accomplished the impossible alone and without support. We tell ourselves that because, since we struggled as we climbed, we must not have had enough help along the way. No one (and I mean not one person) made it to be a loser, let alone a winner by themselves.

Every person that comes into your life is there for your improvement. It simply depends on if you placed people in the proper position to be effective.

The misconception of "<u>being alone makes you strong</u>" is that we believe that this process is never-ending. The entire point of becoming strong only matters when you can fully display your strength publicly. You can be weak alone, but you must be strong in the company of others. This strength allows you to vocalize your beliefs, fight for injustices, negotiate deals, and lead change in your community.

I, at one point in my life, believed myself to have a social anxiety disorder. I did not like to be in big crowds and I dreaded family functions. But this so happens to coincide with times in my life where I was not as positive a person as I would have liked. Simply: I was depressed! Was my depressive state because I had not found a way to interpret the support my family was able to provide or was my inability to effectively garner the support needed the cause of my depression?

Either way, the more I learned to enjoy my own company the more I learned to enjoy the company of others. The more I learned to enjoy the company of others the more I was able to communicate effectively with others. The more I was able to communicate with others the more I realized that the level of support one receives from family and friends is dependent upon one's ability to magnetize that support through ambition, positivity, and communication. Your family is not lazy, good for nothing, dumb or any of these names we hurl mentally at our loved ones. They are uninspired, unmotivated, and in need of a good leader. That can be you.

Scratch that. It needs to be you!

Communication must be honest and open for any business to thrive. Effective communication is something that alludes many families and many businesses. It is the reason why brothers can go years without talking and the reason business relationships can become so strained that it causes partners to split and close a company. How can being alone lead to better communication? Well, the biggest barrier to honest communication is fear. The fear of hurting someone's feelings and/or alienating that individual. Being alone allows you to focus on the ultimate end goal. We must keep the end goal in mind and work towards its reality above all other things.

There are many components to great leadership. A major component is decisive decision-making skills. Being able to have multiple solutions to one problem and not only selecting just one answer but standing firm in your convictions enough to convince others is imperative. Getting to this point comes from being able to think thoroughly through possible outcomes and weighing the opportunity costs. There are many ways to become more decisive but here is where "solitude" shines. Getting away from the commotion and finding some solitude is not a new idea for leaders. In many legendary scripts there are stories of great individuals going away for extended periods of time to pray, fast, or meditate and coming back more focused and stronger in their mission. On top of that, they came back into the fold with a new ability to lead. To have people follow the mission and the vision comes from your being able to articulate the plans, the goals, the rewards, and the end goal.

Let's talk perspective. If we are being truthful to our self we will have to admit that as we work on getting family involved in our personal journey, we become very emotional. In business, emotions will flare but being able to contain or at the very least harness these emotions to be used as fuel is ideal. The benefits of solitude are vast.

Another consideration is being able to place your life into perspective through self-reflection and family-reflection. Can you be angry at an uncle who did not participate in your life growing up once you understand that he had no uncle in his life growing up? How can he be an effective and dependable family member if he never seen that and has no grounds to build on? Maybe in his mind he thought he was being a great uncle. Being able to take a step back and say to yourself "this is bigger than me and my venture at the moment", you start to see the person beyond the family member and beyond the potential customer or supporter. You see an individual who can grow into not only an asset for what you have going on but an asset for an entire community.

Being alone can make you strong only if you are not viewing it as a punishment. If you allow someone or something to place you in a place of isolation, then that can be torture and make you weaker. In even the most trying times, decide for yourself to step back and run through your inventory of skills. Being alone makes you strong for when you are ready to embrace the world. It is you versus you in solitude.

May the best woman/man win!

## Chapter 3

### Learning a New Way.
Family IS business.

Sometimes, in the face of a crisis the successful will bank on what got them to where they are to get them through. They rely on the old way because it is the only way they know. It has worked for so long they believe that it will continue to work. Their lack of diversity stifles their innovation. If that industry, then goes belly up the pundits come out in droves to tell us what we all already know: "the old way wasn't working!".

The change must come from the top down and here's the thing, for you to be successful you must begin to realize that you are the top. It starts with you.

For most of us, we simply play a role. If it takes a village to raise a child. It takes that child to grow up and fulfill a role for the village to survive. We know this even if we dislike the role we inherit. We understand the ramifications of not participating no matter how much we try to ignore or deny it. So, the village survives at the expense of the child. And what happens when the village faces new dangers that no one is prepared for? This is where the decline of the tribe can begin. And when the tribe breaks down there is no village left to raise the children.

When we are stepping outside of our culture or the social norms set for us by our parents and grandparents, in our mind we wrestle with the fact that you are not supposed to do things that are foreign to your tribe. We are naturally built up by family stories and institutions that served our people and communities well for so long. But again, it works until it doesn't work, and the adjustment is never quick enough to stop the descent.

I hope I did not lose you in the allegorical paragraph above. But I say all of that to say: How do we build a village that lends itself to technological and social advancements? My thought is simply finding a new way to engage the members of your village, tribe or family and allow their innate and God giving talents be the driving force in your business endeavors.

The family is not obligated to support you. Remove that notion from your mind and you will have a better night's sleep. If you want your family to be entrepreneurial in their thinking, but you happen to come from an extensive line of factory workers, understand that they do not have the problem, you do. It is never advisable to take someone from one department and toss them into another, in any field, and then get frustrated with them when they fail to live up to expectations. There must be a system of cross training before implementation.

So, what is the new way? Let's work backward from the old way.

The old way consisted of your drive and ambition leading you to focus on this life that you have never seen firsthand but have witnessed in passing, in entertainment or from friends. The life of an entrepreneur. You take this new life to your family and demand that they comply with your vision. Waking up earlier than usual to spend time crafting your product or service, you sacrifice for your dream. Once you have a prototype you expect your family to then spend their hard-earned money on a product that may or may not be inferior to the products available at the local store. These products are products that your family has been purchasing for generations, in some instances, from other companies. You demand that they turn their back on the companies that they normally spend money on. Companies that have spent time, money and effort making members of your family feel like they can trust these products. Not to mention their branding power. I mean, companies can survive for so long off branding alone. And then there is you.

The nephew, niece, cousin, brother who has a history of not finishing projects, dropping out of college, getting divorced, talking bad about friends, drinking and partying, "turning up" on social media, and not being present at family functions or birthday parties.

Who would you choose to trust your money with?

The new way consists of an "intentional familyhood" approach to business and family. Intentional Familyhood means that your approach to winning over your family's business will rival the top brands and companies on the market. Think of what a company does when they have negative press. Think of what a company does when they introduce a new product. Think of what a company does when they put out a bad product. You want to visualize the best companies that are out there.

You will no longer rest on the fact that your mother sent flowers last time Uncle Bob got sick. These flowers will now be from you with concern and sincerity, because if Mr. Johnson & Johnson had to win over Uncle Bob's business that is the approach they would take. Rather it was genuine love or not they would express it to their core customer base. But, this will also build a stronger family. Nobody owes you anything, especially family members. You can't cry about past relationships when you have a present opportunity to improve them. Let's begin the true process of creating a family that supports every effort you put forth.

## **Steps to Intentional Family-Hood**

Treat family members like valued customers. Here is how we do this.

Start with an effort to build customer loyalty. For example, let's say your family comes out in droves to support your new leather shoe shine business because they love you, that love is not going to keep them coming back to spend hard earned money with you especially if your services are subpar and your products are not "worth it". This is the day and age where anyone and everyone can start up a business and their focuses are to take your customers away from you and make them a part of theirs. We can't have that any longer.

- One way to build loyalty is to get hyper-personal. Sending text messages to cell phones monthly thanking customers for their business and letting them know about upcoming sales is a great start. Being that this is family members it will serve a dual purpose. Family instinctively want to help family, but once they believe that you are not serious they are the hardest customer to win back. So, stay on top of them early. Go all out with keeping them in mind, especially if they have spent money with you.

- Another way to build that customer loyalty is to appoint ambassadors. How many times have you not only invited family members to shop with you but also invited them to make money with you and made it easy to do so? Retail stores gain this type of support by offering loyalty rewards where customers can earn points for purchases. Make your family members a part of your loyalty club. Give them rewards like merchandise or let them earn discounts on products. Customers appreciate being recognized by the companies they shop with, why not allow family to feel that same sort of appreciation.

I also suggest being present at as many family functions as possible. For instance, If you were creating a business aimed at senior citizens, you may show up to a retirement community and call a game of BINGO before leaving your business card for potential customers to get in contact with you. Well, the idea is the same here for your family. Continue to give birthday and Christmas presents but use your services as the gift. This allows family the opportunity to test out your product or service and if you are brazened enough to give your business products/services out as a gift it means that you really believe in it. People are reticent to support something that is not supported by the person selling it. Never give a gift of something that your business does from another company. That is the clearest indication for a family customer to stay far away from what you got going on.

The next step is to show your passion for your business venture. Explain the venture in ways that make sense to the family members that you want to garner support from. The thing about big brands is that they make it easy for the consumer to support them and it does not always mean they want your money. Social currency is an amazing thing if properly utilized and understood.

- People are naturally attracted to positivity and excitement. If you are struggling day to day with maintaining your business or spend too much time harping on the negatives you are driving away potential supporters, especially family. Think of it like this: In a best-case scenario you are going to get one or the other from family; either financial support or morale support. Financial support will come if the family believes in you and your product. Moral support will come if a family member continues to have to tell you not to give up or motivate you all the time. You decide how you want to play this out.

- Look the part. Again, we cannot assume that family is somehow excluded from this modern commercial landscape because they are not. Family wants to know that their money is being spent on good products and that they are getting value for the money when they do decide to part with it. At least respect the fact that they work as hard for their money as you work on your business. When you are conducting business, dress like you are conducting business. Use language that you use during normal work interactions. People will respect your business when you do.

- Always aim to be a solution and never a problem. If you are not solving problems with your business, then you might be faced with solving the ultimate problem: finding a job! Take ownership within the family the same way that you take ownership within your company. If you are expecting to have family members be a source of income for you then figure out a way to make their lives easier as an effect of dealing with you. When it comes to your customers, the goal is to solve a problem for them. That should be no different when dealing with family.

Create "believers". Everyone wants to feel appreciated. We all want to know that our voice and opinions are being heard and valued. By transitioning family from supporters to believers, you have an opportunity to bring the family together and a wonderful opportunity to turn your relatives into a financial windfall. A child loves his grandmother because she is the epitome of love. Her home has fewer rules, is more fun, and a lot of time more relaxing. Creating a family away from your family for your family is the goal of turning cousins into customers.

- Create the difference between what you do and what the competition is doing and make it clear and repeatable. Pricing is one thing, but customer service is a driving force of repeat business. Build your company as the one that is different from everything else that is going on based on one thing that is polarizing. In a world where it is said, "Never do business with family," this book is aiming to be polarizing.

- Make solidarity more than about being family. Make it about being a part of a group where everyone in the group benefits from a heightened sense of loyalty. Take solidarity, which oddly enough should be ingrained in every family but is missing 9 out of 10 times and make it cool. People love to be a part of something that they believe in.

- Create a paradox for your family. Make them feel like they are individualistic in their thinking by joining your group. Make them feel like this very old notion that family should support family is somehow a brand-new concept and they are the early adopters.

Be known for your expertise in the area that you are operating in. credibility is not something that is simply given when you are ready to become a business owner or a new leader. It must be earned and normally it takes a long time. On top of that, your family was present for every mistake that you have made in your life. They know that you can be sometimes lazy. They saw you when you were cheating and unfaithful. They have heard a thousand of your hair-brained schemes. You have a mountain to climb when you realize that you are converting people who know the dark side of your life. Take that into account as you journey forward.

- Do not operate it alone. Last chapter we discussed the importance of stepping away to learn to become a better leader. But once you come back around it is time to now be inclusive in the journey and the business. It is ideal to learn your focus area in secrecy. But secrecy does not bode well during the implementation process. Think on this: If you study and learn in silence to be a doctor and you do not receive a degree no one will know that you have skills to practice medicine. We are fearful that someone will take our idea or sabotage our success. The only person who can sabotage your success is you. Open your doors and let nature in.

Build a team and pay them for their time. This is important. A quick google search will pop up tons and tons of information on how to build a winning team. The one thing that should be stressed is family members that are called to be on your team should be compensated just as you would a stranger. These are individuals who you feel have some form of expertise or skill and that should be valuable enough for you to respect it. Always be looking for opportunities for members on your team. Make them the priority and they will make your company the priority.

- Make sure everyone on the team is operating with the same vision and mission in mind. All efforts should be focused in the same direction. There is no time in business, or a strong family, for people to have individualistic thoughts and ideas. Each member is a continuation of the other. When your team is out and about they are representing you. You must make that clear to all, family or not.

- All the great teams have effective communication. In fact, all the great families have excellent communication. Once you can get your team in a collaborative mode and a communicative mindset you open doors for a formidable team to form. Make sure your team understands that wins and losses come down to strategy and conversations.

There are many more steps to take but these are areas that you can start on immediately. Be ready to be a change agent for your family. Stay in character and understand that you have a lot to prove to your family before you should ever think about asking them to purchase or support your dream. Never make your dream someone else's nightmare.

# Chapter 4

## Values & Virtues

Live values, practice virtues.

Virtue is defined as behavior that shows high moral standards. Values are a person's principles or standards of behavior; one's judgment of what is important in life. In business, like family, both values and virtues are important components to success. The one virtue we learn in the average household is patience. Maybe patience is pushed on us so often because it is extremely difficult to be patient with self, others and the process. But the culture of an organization is paramount to its development. Instilling certain values and virtues into family members is what the highly successful and affluent families across America have figured out. How do we translate that level of structure and discipline into our lives?

It is one thing to have a family business, but it is a completely new thing to have a business family. But the big brands treat their employees like families. The employees come to revere the guidance and vision of great leaders. They become defenders, apologizers, supporters, and display a level of love that usually resides within the family context.

Your company values will communicate what is important to your customers. The people that support you will not have to guess what the purpose of your company is. They will be greeted with the consistent message everywhere they turn. This will let your team, whether family or not, understand their role and expectations when representing the company.

The values of a company can inspire people to act. If you can create a value that people identify with it will ultimately encourage them to take positive action. If we are being honest with self, the biggest complaint we have with our family and friends in the initial stages of starting our business is that they do not seem to act when called. Not only do we seek to motivate our family to act we want to know that they are proud of us and impressed by our efforts. We, as people are seeking approval and recognition for our endeavors and our efforts.

The flip on this is that by creating and following values and virtues for your business and your team you keep yourself on track and you keep your brand in the pocket. Excellence is not something that one wakes up and commits by accident. You must be committed to excellence and fully immersed in the process for it to truly work. Take innovation into account; a company and the employees in it are not necessarily going to be innovative if the company does not have an intentional focus on innovation.

In my family, we educate our children on the different indigenous communities throughout the country and the world. The seven Lakota values are big in my household as a jumping off point for learning and living by values. The reason why we instill values in our children at an early age is that we believe that if they imprint it on their hearts, it will guide them for the rest of their lives. With or without our presence. A great company wants that same type of impression on its employees, its partners, the community, and the world. When bringing together your family to do business, keep in mind that they will be your best asset or worse liability. Value them for what they are and respect the individual. Never demand brand loyalty from a person simply because they had the lucky fortune of being born into your bloodline.

## Chapter 5

### Culture

How do the people feel? That's culture.


If you are a small business owner that does constant research on the trends and waves of company culture you will easily see that building a sense of family amongst the team is ideal for growth and sustainability. Have a sit down with a president or executive of a great company, and before long she or he will begin to speak about how they want the culture of their company to "feel like a family" or you may hear, "we are like a family here". So, the question easily becomes this: why do we say not to do business with family if every business wants their company to feel like one?

The easy answer to that question is that we all love our family, but we are sometimes not a fan of the drama that comes along with it. If you could take just the best parts of the family and leave the extracurricular activities out, you would probably have a dynamic workforce and funding source. When you think about it, that is easy to do with strangers that are becoming associates. We all seem to put our best foot forward initially.

Only over time do you begin to see the real person.

So how can you build with family? I have a simple idea: Treat family like strangers and strangers like family. This means be on your best behavior for family and treat a person you just met with the love and respect that you do family. Maybe it is too utopian of a feel, but for a company, it would be ideal.

Understand that you have the leg up on the competition in some areas when you begin a family business. You need to get out in front of any of the barriers to success that comes with working with loved ones. Where the normal business needs to develop an understanding and gather background information on employees, you are fortunate enough to have knowledge of your team from the start. But there is a caveat. People are different when they are in work mode. You want your team to be in work mode when they are doing work. So, do not rely too much on knowing who you're dealing with because you may be quickly surprised.

A Culture is merely a group of intangibles that make up a way of life. Culturally you have the mentality and belief that you are capable of something or you do not. We must consider the idea, that no culture is still a culture and "bad" culture is a driving force almost stronger than "good" culture. Most families are rooted in an idea that hard work leads to the American dream. There is a top 5% for a reason. It is not common to think the way you are thinking. It is even less common to believe that you will be wealthy and leave a family legacy after it is all said and done. So, our goal when working with family or working through family should be to change the culture in as many people lives as possible.

## How to Positively Affect Culture

### Teaching old dogs' new tricks.

Your family culture is the traditions, habits, practices, and values your family has set for itself. It is what makes you unique and allows you to stand apart from other families. It's the identity of your family.

The first thing you want to do is make the culture visible. Great companies have taglines and slogans. What is the slogan of your family business? Make it transcend what you do and make it about who you are. The family get togethers, birthday parties, BBQ's and bonfires must all begin to orbit around this culture. Self-sufficiency is an idea that is not common for people who work jobs. We do someone's work, we buy someone else's products, we allow someone else to teach our children and provide us our health. Make it intentional that you begin to take some of these responsibilities back from others and create your own.

Secondly, you want to create regular rituals and traditions. For instance, having a monthly business meeting with the family where you talk about ideas and strategies or even practicing selling products can help make something like being an entrepreneur seem normal and achievable. Children love doing the same thing over and over because it helps them learn. This type of learning should be encouraged for all. These rituals will also make others feel like they are a part of the process. That does not ever leave us. Making money and doing business with family needs to be normalized and repetitive. This is the type of family time we all should be engaged in.

Another thing you can do is to be elaborate and talk about the culture often. If you are going to be doing a monthly activity, then you should be talking about it weekly and working on it daily. Each person that comes to the table should have a certain vocabulary. Vocabulary meaning verbiage. Verbiage meaning the whole family should be saying and doing the same things as often as possible. This makes culture second nature. Remember a good culture create a good family the same way a good culture creates a good business. They are one and the same.

Finally, as the person taking charge, you must embrace the new culture and follow it as often as possible.

My brother wanted to instill a new culture in our family. His goal was to reconnect us to the roots that made us strong and unique. So, he made our maternal grandmother, who passed away over 20 years ago, God bless her soul and keep her, the beacon of hope for our family. The symbol and icon of our coming together and doing better. He started to call us a tribe after her name. He created terminology that was uplifting. He organized family reunions that were not family reunions but meetings of the minds and icebreakers in approach. I am happy to report that I am still considered a proud "Francinite" and feel like what he accomplished is the beginning of our entire family supporting each other on another level. A business level. An independent level.

You set the tone and you mold the vision. Make it fun and make it doable. People will follow if they are included.

## Chapter 6

### You Are in Control
Power moves from here on out.

A leader is a person that understands his or her position and uses it to make other people better. Leaders share the glorify and is selfish with the blame. When you are bringing together a team, take ownership early on that you are in control of the outcome. It is also imperative that you make your team aware of the things that they have control over. This will make them more confident in their approach and actions.

There is no secret ingredient for bringing people together or making them perform at an elevated level. But, one thing that does always seem to be present in successful teams is the leader being available. I have worked in many offices as well as in retail and in light industrial settings and I always appreciated the "open door" policy and the "walking the floor" atmospheres.

When your team can reach out and touch you when they are struggling, it helps build confidence in their overall performance. This is on you. You could get closer to your family and share moments with them. Share the vision and the goal with them. If they feel like they can rely on you being present in their life you will have a supporter who will show up for your products.

Let's start simply: if your family is not showing up to support your business then you have faulted somewhere in the process. There is a propensity to blame others for our shortcomings especially when it seems like an easy road. But there have been families throughout history who have done it and done it well. So, let's talk about how you can gain confidence in your ability to lead and in turn control the outcomes for your business as it relates to your family.

First things first, you must gain control over your life. If you want to lead others, then take some time to learn how to lead yourself. There are many ways to become a better leader, but you should start by understanding what kind of leader you would like to be and what your leadership style will be. This is different from Chapter 2, where we talk about learning to like your own company. This understanding comes from trial and error, conversation and discussion, and at the end of the day simply getting out there and doing what you say you are going to do. Talk is cheap.

Leadership styles are the characteristics you use when you find yourself in charge. Just because you find that you have a certain style does not mean you have to be married to it. Some find that the style they have developed over time is not the one they want to carry into the future. Learn to spot if these characteristics are helping or hurting you and your relationships.

*Live by Quote: Marry the mission. Date the methods.*

Think about your strengths and weigh them against your weaknesses. Do not try to improve your weaknesses off bat, focus on strengths initially. There are many of leadership style quizzes you can find on the internet. I would encourage you to take one and begin the process of understanding your style.

Once you understand how you lead, it is time to learn how to lead better. *Practice does not make perfect*. **Perfect practice makes perfect**. Your family is witnessing you transform from one of them to *"one of them"*. It is going to take time for your dreams to catch up to their realities or vice versa. Encouraging your family to stay creative in their own lives will help speed up the process. We all spent summer nights staring at the skies with our cousins talking about the big houses we were going to buy and the fancy vacations we were going to take. Call up your cousin and begin to dream again. This time with the intention of leading them to a place where their dream can be realized. It may help them understand why you believe your business can be successful. Remember passion is contagious. The more you have of it the more you pass it on.

When we started GBRTGalaxy in 2016 we had this vision and no supporters. Our family had witnessed us cruise through life and we made all sort of excuses as to why no one wanted our products. The last thing we were ready to admit to was that we were the problem or rather that our style was the issue. When my partners Zachary Van Harris and Jason Vaughan decided that they were stepping away from the business, I had time to sit with this behemoth.

We had created a multimedia company with RocNation as our model for comparison. As I looked around I realized that the low hanging fruit, i.e. family and friends seemed to be out of reach. And so, this became my focus. Turning family and friends into our first customers. The marketing plan was easy. Help them create their businesses and they will soon understand that businesses need supporters. It was a remarkable success. Not only did we get more followers on our social media, but we had business partners and partnering businesses. Not all those businesses reached fruition, but everyone was riding on the waves of ownership. It was inspiring. It is truly better to give than to receive because once you begin to give out the right energy you will receive it right back. Start giving today!

Leadership comes down to making a very few changes to your communication style and thought process. By taking a problem and viewing it as an opportunity you continue to move forward in your development. Taking ownership of outcomes make you more decisive and confident as well. We have all spent our lives putting out family problems. Working with family is not much different. Very small miscommunications can cause big impacts in our families. The same can be said for small businesses and its staff. Being a better communicator is another thing that you need to take control over and is critical to be mindful of.

A leader must develop the tools to respond to a situation instead of reacting. Reacting to the situation almost always leads to negativity when it comes to leading others. A good leader has the tools to communicate what is needed in others that will lead them to take the correct positive action. Developing your communication style starts with being able to be an effective listener. In America, we do not listen to what the person is saying we listen for our chance to speak. This needs to be changed immediately.

<u>Transformational leadership</u> should focus on providing your team with one on one communication. During

these conversations always, express care and concern for the individual and where they are in their life.

Control is a good thing to have if you have control over yourself. Once you assume control understand that many will fight for your vision. Make it clear and plain for them to follow. Always ask yourself if you are creating a barrier-free way to share your experience with your family. Some have no idea of how products are developed, or organizations built, it is in your hands to educate them and groom them for the future.

There are other things you can do to be a better leader for your family and your business like:
- work next to your team
- show your passion for their success
- listen and communicate intently
- keep your attitude in check
- pull them in to contribute.

These things will connect your family to your business mission like never.

## Chapter 7

### Bring Them Out

To al my supporters… Thank you.

Now that you have educated your family, empowered your supporters, improved your understanding of yourself, and learned your leadership style, it is now time for the ask. How do you now get your family to come out and support your business? There is no right way to approach launching a business. There are many people selling videos on how to do this and how to do that, but the reality of the situation is not one thing works for every person. The best thing you can do at this point is trust that you have done all the legwork to satisfaction and live with the results.

Now that you have everyone waiting for the release, it is time to start promoting and using the correct wording for launch. This may not be the sole factor for why people shop with you, but it does help. Think of how you promote and make sure it is in line with culture and has meaning. Nike and its "Just Do It" tag is perfect. It basically makes the buyer go from contemplating to action in every aspect of life. Even shopping. Why spend all day thinking about buying this $100 hoodie? Just do it!

When we began to focus on "intentional familyhood" with GBRTGalaxy we knew that we needed something that stood out and moved our base. After some back and forth we trademarked and launched our T-Shirt line "Good Brothers Run Together" ©. This, we felt, had a strong meaning and built on the foundation of our family. We wavered on if we were isolating our potential women fanbase but decided to HAVE an all-male base was better than what we currently had: no base at all! This was our talking point and it really gave our company a hook. We enjoyed much success with this motto/slogan/tagline/mantra. A small nugget of truth: Women actually loved the slogan just as much as men. We overthought something we now live by: Dope is Dope! People like Dope things.

Giving away merchandise is also a natural way to get people interested in the products and the company. Also, free merchandise turns families and friends into walking billboards. If you can get a person who has some social influence, whether online or in the public, to wear a T-Shirt or post about your product you are likely to capture the attention of their audience. Make sure that you are being strategic with your giveaways. You would not want to waste money or resources in an area that does not return dividends.

Taking pictures and putting them in view of your potential supporters is another way to get them to come out and support. Using social tools like Twitter and Instagram is a way to not only get the items out to the public but it also shows your family and friends that you are seriously invested in your business. Always remember the motto: Treat family like strangers and strangers like family. You must sell the product to your inner circle the same if not more than you sell it to complete strangers. There is nothing wrong with this. In fact, embrace it. Since there is already genuine love in most families, getting a family member to buy into you early will guarantee you a customer for the life of your venture. If you treat them fairly.

Don't just be a salesman, provide the content that is needed to make your input matter. One way to do this is by commenting on sites and joining in on the conversation. Get out of your comfort zone and comment on everything from videos to blogs, discussion boards, articles, and forums. All of these can get your name out there and have people coming out to support you. The thing about a family, which is really the same for most, is that many of them want to support things that are already being supported on a major scale. If you are looking for a foolproof way to get your family involved and interested, I would suggest growing your presence as one option.

Now here is the deal and one that many will cringe when they read: BE ANNOYING. Family will support you, but sometimes they need to be invited out to the party. You must bombard your friends and families. Even though you may feel as if this book is about how to galvanize your family to support you, at the end of the day family wants family to succeed. This book is more about how you allow, yes allow your family to support you. You must email them, text them, share the URL, FB message them, etc. etc. etc. and let them know that you are open for business. A lot of time family will tell you that they had no idea that you were starting a business even if you have told them multiple times. Keep on them and do not stop until they buy something. Even if its just a cup of coffee to tell you how bad of an idea you have. Assuming you have done everything, you are required to do, it is the least that they can do. Do not take no for a no! Most people have to be told something multiple times before they say yes. Take this as a test. Give it the <u>power of seven approach</u>. Plan to ask 7 times before you call it quits.

Do not quit. That is the best advice I can give you and should be in your mind always. The truth of the matter is that no matter how good the product is nobody is going to buy the product initially they are going to buy into you. Have you given them enough to go on? When something does not work try something else and see how that goes. Put yourself out there. Your family can be critical and very judgmental, but that is their way of preparing you for the real world. I cannot stress this enough: Your family loves you and they are not out to destroy your dream. Always remember that. If you keep that in mind you can always reflect on maintaining control of the situation. Ask yourself: Have I done enough for myself and my business. Is my product good enough? What more can I do to encourage my family to support me?

If you feel as if your family does not believe in you then ask yourself this: Do you believe in yourself? If yes, then forge ahead with unwavering faith and belief. It will work!

# Chapter 8

## Joy is Currency

"love is something if you give it away, you end up having more" -Malvina Reynolds

"The rich don't work for money." I read this during my journey in becoming a leader and small business owner. This pertains to individuals that use tax breaks and debt to remain wealthy. That is a book for another day. With the economy in constant flux, we must learn how to make money while we are not working. Investments, assets, etc. etc. is ideal. But for this chapter, we are talking about simply being happy to be waking up and doing what you are doing. This idea is to live in the now. Enjoy the work. Finding something that pays you the more you do it. Not in money. <u>Make joy your currency.</u>

Imagine having a family business that is fully supported by the people that you love and trust. The same people that you shared your dream with as a young kid is now sitting in boardrooms and on conference calls with you. That is an amazing feat to accomplish and it should be embraced as such.

Through this book, we talked about all the steps you need to take to become better and the strategies one can implement to get the most out of your family. You motivated your followers. If at this moment your major concern is making money, then you stopped paying attention at some point. All this building up is to make you a better leader. Bringing together people to accomplish something greater than the sum of the parts does not always equal money instantly. But what this does do is make you and your team/family more impactful and position everyone involved for a brighter future.

While there are many pitfalls to starting a business that depends on family support there are also many benefits, one being stability. Families are natural teams. They have spent decades teaching each other.

Familiarity helps the natural process of going from idea to implementation. Families have a knack for working together to figure out the toughest of jobs.

Think about the last-minute family reunions or funeral arrangements for a family member who does not have insurance. When in trouble, families come together like no other can. Someone cooks, someone opens their home, someone makes the calls, another person brings the music... it is naturally impressive and inspirational. How can we bottle up that energy and utilize it in a non-emergency situation? Create joy!

Remember why you started out on this journey. At no point did you think to yourself, "I can't wait to work for myself so that I can be miserable". Now, working for yourself is one of the most difficult things that a person can attempt to accomplish. But the joy of being in the moment overtakes the struggles. If the negatives outweigh the positives, then you may have to refocus on the actual goal to make sure you chose the correct path.

Let's talk about the joys of owning your own business:

- more than 80% report being happier than they were when they had a job
- 88% believe that their future is brighter
- More than half exercise more than before they started their own business
- 74% eat healthier
- 50% wear whatever they want to work (including pajamas)
- 60% work with a close relative

There are many that will tell you that to make it you have to be ready to sacrifice family, friends, sleep, and play time. While this may be true in a lot of respects we are working towards a different goal. How do we achieve success while not sacrificing the things that got us started but also finding a way to make them more a part of the journey? This goes back to "Intentional Familyhood" and making family an integral part of your business. There are companies that make friendships a driving part of the company culture. Some of the greatest organizations have figured out how to make playtime a part of the work schedule. In every instance, the leader of these great companies set out to be intentional. The same fall at your feet. Sacrifice your ego before you sacrifice family, friends, and fun.

## The Three F's
## Family, Friends, & Fun

Making family a priority is becoming more and more accepted by professionals. For a long time, men and women were forced to decide between a family (a healthy family that is) and a career. Now, this might have been more a struggle for women because of childbirth, but men were also up against it. Thank goodness we have evolved and matured in our thinking on work and life balance. Traveling across the globe in sales does not make for a healthy father-child bond. The best of companies is now offering work/life balance as an attraction for top talent. When you become a self-employed individual, you have full control over that balance. It is still a tough thing to balance, but it at least puts the control in the right hands: your own.

Working in an office setting where people are friendly and are having fun is always a better place to be. On the flip side of that, working in a toxic environment where people are constantly bickering and at each other necks is hell. So, since we are witnessing companies being mindful of hiring individuals that fit company culture we see that you should not have to sacrifice friends when you start your business. You simply must find a way to make your friends an important part of the process and the overall business in general.

Of course, things change once money and responsibility come into play, so I always want to be sure to remind people that not all your friends are created equal. Find the individuals that have a certain knack for business and have displayed a history of integrity, work ethic, and persistence. These traits are not visible in all people. If you take your time and survey your group, you will be able to separate the wheat from the chaff.

Who wants to work where they are not having fun? Not too many. There is an idea that instead of following your passion you start a business that fits your idea of having fun. This may seem a little irresponsible, but if you think about it in context, why would you not be passionate about something you consider to be an enjoyable time. I used to watch a lot of sports and I never understood why players thanked God for the ability to play the game. I was only half hearing what they meant. What they are saying is thank God that they can play a game, get paid, and be rich living the life that they dreamed of as as child. Who wouldn't want that to be true?

Always take time to think about exactly why you want to start a business and what is the purpose of your business. Once you figure out the why, then work on the what. I would encourage you to stay flexible and basically have fun. Sometimes people start businesses to change the world or because they want to make a lot of money. Both of those are good reasons but none is better than to be able to simply enjoy life and live the way you want. Think about the favorite thing of yours to do when you were a child. Now imagine you can get paid millions of dollars to do that every day for the rest of your life. See? Isn't that motivating enough?

## **Making others Happy**

Whether we are talking about family, friends, or strangers your goal in any business is to make others happy. Your product is being sold to satisfy a need. Your service is being marketed to help a person reach another level. Any business not in the "make our customer happy" lane is not going to be a business for long.

The key to happiness is making others happy. Why?
- You can see the joy that you spread and like they say a smile is contagious.
- You know deep down that you did a good deed and that just feels good.
- You get what you give out. The rule of cause and effect is real. Reap what you sow!

Simple ways to make others happy:
- Give compliments to the people that your work with.
- Do not take anything for granted.
- Show gratitude for even the smallest things.
- Encouragement. Keep others around you inspired.

- Share some life lessons and advice.
- Listen to them vent.
- Smile. Remember it is contagious.

Happiness happens to those that are making it happen for others.

# Chapter 9

## Representing

Make it an honor to represent family in public.

We discussed our shortcomings. We dealt with those shortcomings. We talked about the barriers to support. We removed those barriers to make it easy for families to support us. We moved from expecting our families to purchase our products and services to work for our numbers. We grew in our leadership. We even prioritized what was most important in our journey. There is nothing more important than joy.

Now it is time for us to step out on all these things and represent.

## Five things to consider when representing the family business

1. You must have the mindset that it is a privilege and an honor to represent your brand. Your family is your brand. Your brand is your family. Remember that the public is judging your character and your attitude. If you are going to impact change you must be aware that this automatically makes you a role model and public figure. Consider those days that your mother reminded you that how you act reflects upon the whole house. This narrative never changes. Your actions can improve or dramatically hurt the business and the family.

2. Dress to impress. Now you do not have to always be in suits, but you should be sure to be clean and groomed when in public. Obviously, your level of grooming is up to the standard that you've set for yourself and your team/family. But the way you're dressed says a lot about you especially when you are on "company" time. Taking your time to being well groomed, good hygiene, and dressing professionally at events goes a long way to earning respect amongst your peers.

3. Be sure to know what you are selling and understand the market. The last thing you want to do is put all this effort into your startup and get into a conversation about a field that you know nothing about. Consumers are super savvy, and they are going to be testing you to make sure that you are up to date with your knowledge. Why buy from you if you don't even know the basics of your industry. Imagine buying macaroni from a person who does not know what's in the recipe.

4. Improve your people skills. It is no excuse for you to be bad at interacting at this stage. If you have no interpersonal skills and you have no interest in improving them, please stay behind the scenes. Miscommunication has been the fall of many great families, businesses, and relationships throughout the annals of time. You cannot survive in this climate thinking that the consumer already knows what they want to buy. While that might be true you have to understand that some people, in fact, most people want to

be educated by the people they are buying from. It is up to you to be able to sell them on the things that they are not privy to.

5. The secret to selling is listening. We do not spend a lot of time perfecting our product to sell it to ourselves. We hope that once we put together our wonderful product the public will see its value and purchase it. We must consider what the market is calling for and what people are requesting. Being bullheaded and sticking to your guns can cause you to be responsible for the failure of the family business. Some will decide that they would rather work alone than to be held back by restraints. Those people will soon be back to help the ship that is focused on powerful impact. It is ok to let people go and test their theories. The things that work, work because they always worked. So, understand that the overall mission and goal is bigger than your personal aspirations and your ego. There are a lot of lonely people that were "right"!

Representing the family name like representing the family business is a thing of honor and privilege. It should not be taken for granted. There have been many people who have come before you and sacrificed and gave everything they had for your future. These are people in some instances that did these things without even knowing you personally. I am always impressed by family crests. I think that they serve as a visual reminder of the family brand. This gives countless generations of members of that family pride and identity. It gives them something to live up to. Instilling leadership in your family at an early age will instill some of these same traits.

Family culture is important for numerous reasons. The thing I value most in culture is the vision. When you have an entire group of people wholeheartedly invested in one vision it makes that road that much easier to travel down. Having one vision can give all members of the family consistency and stability. This allows them to stand for the things that they believe in and speak out against the things that they do not.

What do you stand for?

What do you stand against?

Which questions was harder to answer? Whichever it was doesn't matter, the basis of these questions and the way you answered generally comes from the culture of your family. The things that you value and the way you express those ideas are not original thoughts. They are an accumulation of many different ideas over time that you have been exposed to. You have been groomed to feel and react to situations the way you do by family and friends.

Business strategy is defined simply as a firm's high-level plan for reaching specific business objectives. These strategies are considered successful when they lead to growth, competitive position and increased financial performance. There are many factors and different forms of this strategy. Again, a different book for a different time. Bottom line, these strategies are put in place to make the company successful short and long term. You can use certain principles to position yourself to achieve better results from these strategies. What would a family strategy look like?

Let's define a family strategy.

A family strategy is a family's high-level plan for reaching specific family objectives. These strategies are considered successful when they lead to spiritual growth in the family members, increased output in the family members performance, and boosted confidence in each member when operating in public.

Here are our principles:

- Be unique not the best.

Being the best family is subjective and very difficult to quantify. In fact, this can lead to confusion. Therefore, it is never ideal to try and keep up with the Jones's. They have their own thing going. Figure out the best way for you and your family to operate and go with it. There is no one that can do you better than you.

- Know your family before creating your strategy.

You want to position everyone to be successful. Creating a plan without considering everyone's strengths and weaknesses is a recipe for disaster. Make sure that your plan challenges everyone just a little as well as make it easy for everyone to succeed in their respective areas.

- Give the members a choice.

At the end of the day, while we would love for everyone to buy into the dream, we must understand that not everyone wants to be a part of it nor should everyone be a part of it. Leave the door open for individuals to decide their own path. This includes the little ones. Give them the option. There is nothing that spells trouble like forced participation.

- Teach all how to say "No" Often.

It is good to give the family a vision, but it is imperative that you empower them with the word "no" or "no thank you". If your family is not able to say "no" to others and to you then they have not fully bought into the strategy. Good strategy requires members to know what they will and will not do.

- Keep the family moving in the right direction.

Yes, keep them moving in the right direction but more importantly, you must keep them moving period. Being that you have a strategy for your family means that you are amongst the elite in "Intentional Familyhood", but that also means that you are now in unfamiliar territory. When in doubt put your head down and forge ahead. Remind the family that you have not got this far to freeze up.

Once you have mastered these principles, you can then begin to put together and implement your family strategy. This is a guide for your entire family that will lead you to the next level of the journey. A family strategy leading to economic success is ideal, but also one that leads everyone to be their greatest version. There are many reports that suggest family businesses that install a family strategy with binding rules and agreements are more successful overall. There are even families that have created a family constitution that all members agree to. They benefit from greater family peace and increases the emotional relationships of the family and the family business.

I really encourage you to take some time and consider each member when putting together any kind of agreement. It is vital that everyone feels that they have a great chance at succeeding in the system.

## Conclusion

When I sat down to write this book I must admit I did not fully know how I would capture the struggles and frustrations of failed family support. But once I sat with the idea I began to realize that I was expecting something from my family that I did not expect to receive from anyone else. I was expecting automatic support. In a way, I disrespected their work and achievements by assuming that everything in their life should drop for me because I was in need. And there's that word, right? NEED! Those that are in the greatest need are more likely to declare how they do not need anyone.

This book did not take long to put to paper because the core of it I have been writing for my entire life. It began to flow once I understood the simple notion that I have control over my outcomes.

Zayn Malik says, "It's nice to look out and see your family supporting you."

I couldn't agree more. It is very rewarding to know that the people that really matter to you believe in you so much that they are willing to support you. But for me, there must be more to it. Coming from a community that is not necessarily the greatest at spending money with each other, I wanted to start a movement. I did not want to make it a bad thing to not support family, but to make it an incredibly remarkable thing to support family.

"Support what you love instead of bashing what you hate"

We have become so accustomed to the idea that family should bend over backward for us that we completely absolve ourselves of any fault findings. Mighty fine beam in thine eye there! We are complacent in the relationships that we have cultivated over the years and we must take that power back. There are no bad families only missed opportunities and poor communications.

Family is by default designed to support you. So, if you get them to come out and support you on that alone, you have failed. That's nothing. It is not enough. You have not lived up to any potential you and your family have nor, did you push the culture forward. But if you can let's say get family to work together, build co-brands, teach and educate each other on economics, show and prove the power of investments and group economics and the dynamics of circulating the dollar then you have improved on the design.

"family is not an important thing. It's everything." – Michael J. Fox

From this moment I want all the readers to approach your business model with "Intentional Familyhood". Meaning that you will begin to show up to parties and functions and support family members and their children. You will listen to their struggles and dissect their concerns. When you present your product or service it will be something that they need and want and not something that you are forcing them to buy from you out of "love". You will market to your closest friends and families with the same vigor as Coca-Cola and Johnson & Johnson does. It will make the difference between one "love" purchase and a lifelong customer/partner.

If we don't take the time to educate our family on all things business related, we stand to lose them down the line to another fancy company with the bells and whistles. Branding is hard to break once it is established. So, you must begin now with instilling culture and values in the little ones. Never make your journey their burden. Think further than to your next payday and think 10 years into the future. How will these chickens come home to roost?

In the Jewish community, they talk about failing forward. While everyone assumes that Jewish communities are immune from bad business, even in their community a good portion of new businesses fails. The idea of failing forward is a motivational life lesson that prepares you for things to come. Keep in mind that you do not lose. You either win or you learn.

*The whole books sum up to this: If you can find a way to make people matter you will never be in* **need.**

*Eirene means peace!*

# ABOUT THE AUTHOR

Intentional Familyhood is a simple idea that focuses on your approach with family when it comes to business or change.

Eddie Jaroul is long time Nonprofit Leader with background in Program Development, Diversity Training and Inclusion Engagement. After spending his life as the middle child, whose sole purpose was putting out fires between siblings, he shares his ideas of what may work when dealing with family and business.

He lives in Western Michigan with his wife and lovely children.

*Educating others starts with educating self.*

www.ingramcontent.com/pod-product-compliance
Lightning Source LLC
Chambersburg PA
CBHW052335220526
**45472CB00001B/431**